FROM A DISTANCE

JULIE GOLD

illustrated by JANE RAY

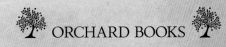

ORCHARD BOOKS

ORCHARD BOOKS
96 Leonard Street
London EC2A 4RH

ISBN 1 86039 637 2

This edition first published in Great Britain in 1998

Special thanks to Peter W. Primont, George Edward Regis, Burt Stein and Alan Koenig, and above all to
Nanci Griffith.

Love and thanks to Clara and Ellen Temple for additional artwork.

AN ALBION BOOK

Designed by Emma Bradford
Typeset in Weiss

Typesetting by York House Typographic, London
Colour origination by Culver Graphics, High Wycombe
Printed in Hong Kong / China by South China Printing Co. (1988) Ltd.

Connect Humanitarian Agency has supplied new and donated books to all the major libraries
and schools throughout Bosnia Herzegovina.
Further information on Connect can be obtained from
20 St. Leonard's Bank, Edinburgh EH8 9SQ

For children of all ages all around the world
JULIE GOLD

and for
CONNECT HUMANITARIAN AGENCY
working in Bosnia
JANE RAY

FROM A distance
The world looks blue and green
And the snow-capped mountains white

From a distance
The ocean meets the stream
And the eagle takes to flight

From a distance, there is harmony
And it echoes through the land

It's the voice of hope
It's the voice of peace
It's the voice of every man

From a distance
We all have enough
And no one is in need
There are no guns, no bombs, no diseases
No hungry mouths to feed

From a distance, we are instruments
Marching in a common band
Playing songs of hope
Playing songs of peace
They're the songs of every man

God is watching us, God is watching us
God is watching us from a distance

From a distance
You look like my friend
Even though we are at war
From a distance, I can't comprehend
What all this war is for

From a distance, there is harmony
And it echoes through the land

It's the hope of hopes
It's the love of loves
It's the heart of every man

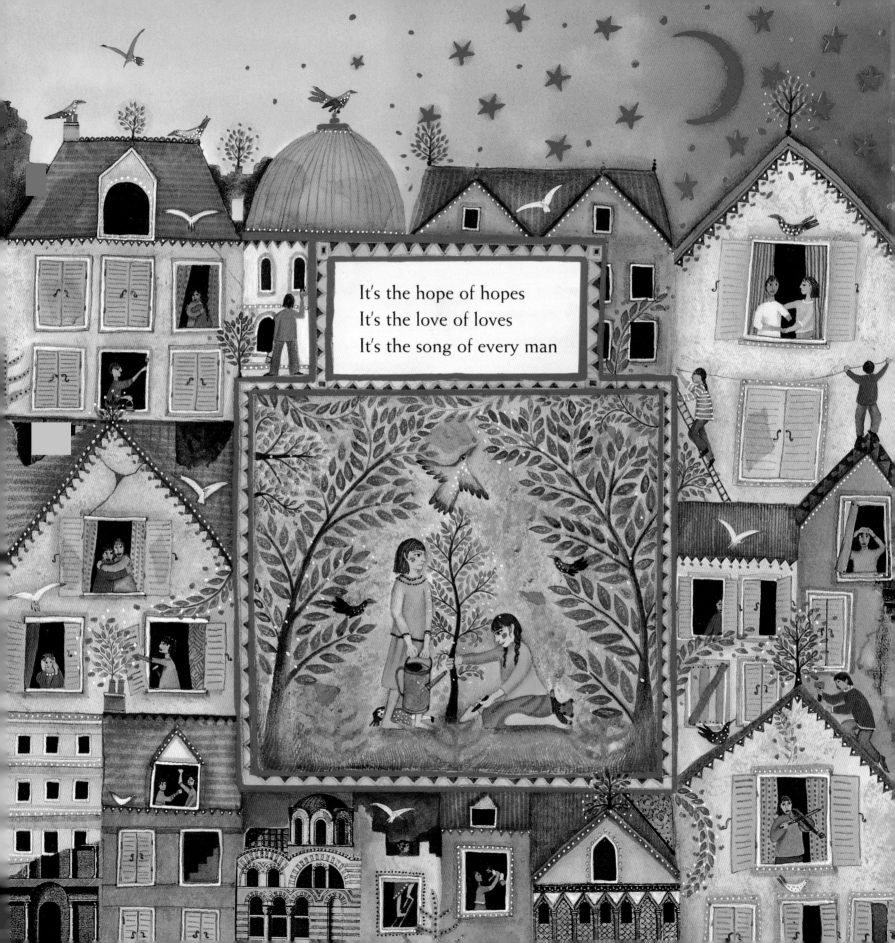

It's the hope of hopes
It's the love of loves
It's the song of every man

From a distance
The world looks blue and green
And the snow-capped mountains white
From a distance
The ocean meets the stream
And the eagle takes to flight

From a distance, there is harmony
And it echoes through the land
It's the voice of hope
It's the voice of peace
It's the voice of every man

From a distance
We all have enough
And no one is in need
There are no guns, no bombs, no diseases
No hungry mouths to feed

From a distance, we are instruments
Marching in a common band
Playing songs of hope
Playing songs of peace
They're the songs of every man

God is watching us, God is watching us
God is watching us from a distance

From a distance
You look like my friend
Even though we are at war
From a distance, I can't comprehend
What all this war is for

From a distance, there is harmony
And it echoes through the land
It's the hope of hopes
It's the love of loves
It's the heart of every man

It's the hope of hopes
It's the love of loves
It's the song of every man

I TRULY BELIEVE that when you love what you do, you do it with God. I love music. I love writing songs.

I grew up in the sixties and I have vivid memories of all that was happening in the world then: the Vietnam War, the Civil Rights Movement, the Women's Movement, the Space Programme, the Beatles. When I recall those memories, I recall the songs that were popular at the time, and it's as if those songs actually orchestrated those events. All my memories come with a soundtrack.

I wrote "From a Distance" in 1985. It was the culmination and outpouring of all my vivid memories and experiences. I am honoured to receive all the loving responses it has elicited over the years, and I hope I am managing that love in a responsible way. It thrills me to think that a little song I wrote in a one-room apartment right before my thirtieth birthday has brought so much joy to children of all ages all around the world.

Maybe some day we will all live in a world that has no guns, no bombs, and no diseases – that's my hope of hopes.

JULIE GOLD